Anna Adams was born in West London in 1926. She studied art at Harrow Art School and Hornsey College of Art, and in 1947 married the painter Norman Adams. She has worked as an art teacher, a casual farm labourer, a pottery designer, and latterly as a freelance writer, while still drawing, painting and making terracottas.

Since the mid–1950s Anna Adams has lived with her husband and two sons in Manchester, Yorkshire, Tyneside and the Hebrides. She now spends part of the year in Ribblesdale, Yorkshire, and part in London, where her husband is Professor of Painting at the Royal Academy Schools. Her most recent publications, combining prose and poetry, are *Island Chapters* (1991) and *Life on Limestone* (1994).

ANNA ADAMS

Green Resistance

NEW AND SELECTED POEMS

London
ENITHARMON PRESS
1996

First published in 1996
by the Enitharmon Press
36 St George's Avenue
London N7 0HD

Distributed in Europe
by Password (Books) Ltd.
23 New Mount Street
Manchester, M4 4DE

Distributed in the USA and Canada
by Dufour Editions Inc.
PO Box 7, Chester Springs
PA 19425-0007, USA

ISBN 1 870612 57 4

Typeset in 10pt Bembo by Bryan Williamson, Frome,
and printed by The Cromwell Press, Wiltshire

CONTENTS

5

PUBLICATIONS BY ANNA ADAMS

A Journey Through Winter (Manchester Institute of Contemporary Art, 1969)
Parabola (Headland, 1975)
Unchanging Seas (Headland, 1978)
A Reply to Intercepted Mail (Peterloo Poets, 1979)
Island Chapter (Littlewood, 1983)
Brother Fox (MIDNAG, 1983)
Dear Vincent (Arc Publications, 1986)
Trees in Sheep Country (Peterloo Poets, 1986)
Six Legs Good (Mandeville, 1987)
Angels of Soho (Royal Academy, 1988)
Nobodies (Peterloo Poets, 1990)
Island Chapters (Arc Publications, 1991)
Life on Limestone (Smith Settle, 1994)
Green Resistance: New and Selected Poems (Enitharmon, 1996)

ACKNOWLEDGEMENTS

Acknowledgements are due to Harry Chambers of Peterloo Poets, who has stood by the poet for many years, and to John Killick, who made the initial selection of poems for this volume.

Some of the new poems in the final section of the book were first published in the following magazines and publications: *Aquarius 19/20*, *Emotional Geology* (Stride), *The Green Book, Iron, The North, Orbis, Pennine Poets' Chapbook* (1995), *PN Review, Poetry Book Society Anthology 2, Poetry Durham, Poetry Review, Stand*.

To Norman

BLURB

Think of caseworms in their streams
    gathering stray bric-a-brac –
    sandgrain, leafscrap, broken stick,
to disguise their tender forms:

Binding tesserae of trash
    close, to make a carapace –
    intricate mosaic face –
covering near-naked flesh.

Think of poets in the street
    finding unconsidered snatches –
    phrases overheard – for patches
to be stitched into a coat

That close-fits transparent thought.
    They obsessively construct
    intellectual artefacts,
Babel-towers to support

Flickerings of inner flame,
    shielding it from unkind winds,
    circumstances, obtuse minds,
housing fire in name on name –

Images purloined from Dream –
    using what they hear, touch, see,
    to embody mystery.
Poems swim upstream through Time,

Keeping in the present tense,
    hearing still the ever-young
    poets of archaic tongue
making one harmonious sense.

Permutations of the rhymes
    work like genes in DNA
    keeping poetry OK,
constantly renewing themes

in contemporary dress:
    Death and Love, and Love and Death,
    Poets' truth, till our last breath,
sings our dole of consciousness.

THE OXFAM COAT

I do not wear this coat to be admired,
not even to be seen;
it is for seeing from.
I am a walking look-out post, attired

in mist and dead-leaf coloured camouflage –
a watcher's hide, a property
avisible as poverty,
as inconspicuous as middle-age.

It must have needed thirty years, at least,
to reach this natural state
and yet remain an artefact
that keeps me warm. To ditch it would be waste.

It cost me twenty pence. Good Harris cloth,
springy as heather turf:
it has outworn the striding farmer's wife
its cut suggests. Her scarecrow bones are earth.

It has outworn its power to startle birds
and has become a rough
looking-glass fibre stuff
chameleon, reflecting winter woods.

That matted sheep – potential bale of wool
on knitting needle legs –
sees me as sheep. Those twigs
sense me as bark-skinned tree if I stand still.

Obliterated by this patina
I travel incognito. Outline blurs.
Brown dyes revert to lichen, bracken, furze;
I register on no man's retina.

Extract from
A REPLY TO INTERCEPTED MAIL

A Verse-Letter to W. H. Auden, verses 73 to 79

This screed about my distant past unrolled
    like miles of spiky wire, out of my pen –
entangling foolscap sheets – because I told
    you my address, and wanted to explain
    how I arrived so slowly. If I'd been
more disciplined I might have found my path
through the dark wood before I brushed with Death.

I read a lot, I wrote a bit, I thought –
    but disconnectedly – I worked for cash:
I drew, I made small sculptures, and I taught,
    and had acquired two children when the crash
    from happiness, the lash of Nemesis,
dropped me from sunlight – woman's summertime –
to punishment – it seemed – for lack of crime.

I'm trying to be honest and extract
    the essence of what happened from events;
to winnow grains of truth from chaff of fact,
    and not pretend to feeling or to sense
    more than is mine – nor claiming innocence.
But back in 1960, suddenly
shipwrecked into the Leeds Infirmary –

on the receiving end of pity, ill,
    humiliated, and afraid to die –
I dreamed that on my cottage window-sill
    there crawled a captive Brimstone butterfly
    that battered at the room's impervious eye
with frantic wings, to reach the sun outside,
while all the time the door stood open wide.

This meant, to me, that I should write much more,
　　that my soul could find egress through the word;
out of my cottage skull it was the door,
　　and in my head, repeatedly, I heard
　　your song for William Yeats, the greater bard.
'Time worships language, and forgives,' you said,
'all those by whom it lives.' I heard, and prayed

for a reprieve. Invigilator Death,
　　who had sat quietly, and unobserved,
in my life's room where the supply of breath
　　would last a hundred years, I thought, had heaved
　　himself out of his chair, and his jaw moved.
'Time's up in this exam. Put down your pen.
Hand in the papers you have just begun,'

he ordered. I looked at my nearly blank
　　examination papers; begged for time;
and time was granted, at a price. I thank
　　the National Health Service for each line
　　I've made since then, unless the medicine
was poetry, my spirit's energy,
new positiveness, self discovery.

WREN-SERMON, OR SMALLEST IS SACRED

The flightless bipeds, ponderously slow
    as insubstantial trolls of cumulus
    that loll about the table of the world,
emerge from house to garden, come and go
        while I, as quick as blinking, quick as light,
        dart out of sight.

Obtuse beyond belief, they think I am
    a flying leaf, a shadow, russet rag,
    a mouse run to its crevice in the crag
which shelters me among the armoured game
        that scuttles, quick as winking, quick as light,
        out of my sight.

Quicker than I, the summer hoverfly
    changes its airy stations. Glassy wings
    sustain, invisibly, its humming stance
until it shifts, quite unpredictably,
        to hang a foot away, as quick as shot,
        first here, then not.

The frantic gnats must think it vast and slow,
    but are themselves composed of energies
    like instantaneous eternities:
light particles that shuttle to and fro
        as quick as inspiration, cheating thought,
        setting the table out.

THE DISMANTLING OF THE
YELLOW HOUSE AT ARLES

Theo, your goodness remains
though your kindness has come to nothing.
Full of remorse and grief
I pack up the pictures and studies.
The shelter for comrades in art –
furnished so hopefully
with sunflowers, starry skies,
cornfields and cypresses –
is wrecked.
                  To live alone
again, is a horror to me.
I cannot shift for myself.
I may join the Foreign Legion
to live at peace, under rules;
couldn't I paint in the barracks
as well as in the asylum?
Unrecognised, I have been
a foreign legionnaire –
deserted, not a deserter –
almost all my life.

Unheated, after the flood
which came within feet of the walls,
then locked up by the police,
my studio decomposed.
The plaster was oozing with wet
and some studies were flaking off:
for even pictures fade
like flowers. Painting is madness
and not the real life.

Dear little sister, avoid
the snare of art: but we must
love wholly that which we love,
and I could do nothing else.
So, having no wife of my own
I waited my turn in the brothel
and watched the world's wedding pass by.

Now painting must be my home.
(The magpies and the wrens
should be numbered among the artists;
their homes are works of art.)

I have made the sunflowers mine
and when I had painted them
I looked for their contrast and equal
and I said: 'It is the cypress.'
I made the cypresses mine
while cypress flames possessed me;
I burned in their smoke-black towers
stirred by the summer mistral.
And have you seen the olives?
Silver turns green, turns silver,
under the spell of the sky.
The olive groves rustle of secrets –
immensely ancient, and far
too beautiful to be painted.

My eyes are at work again
like organs of generation.
Emotion, in front of nature,
can overcome my reason.
I enter into the landscape,
lacking those beams in the eye
that bar out too much of the real
and keep the mind in its place.
A fortnight of helplessness:
then I can paint with calm
and logical brushstrokes: calm,
and trying to make it true.
This truth is so dear to me
I cannot let go and compose
pure music in colour, preferring
to paint as though making shoes.

I am losing my fear of madness:
an illness, like any other:
more speakable than the clap;
and love is a microbe too –

so I read – and also this painting
is loving with eyeballs and brush.

The painter's house is all windows –
unframed, uncurtained, glassless –
and the windows remain wide open
and all must have two–way views
into and out of my mind.

TOTES MEER

by Paul Nash: 1940–41

This picture is of waste. No victory
gloats in the absent eye that we make ours
by seeing what it saw. But tragedy
is not stressed either; we may keep our tears.

No beggar whimpers for them, we are shown
no scars, no mutilations, no burnt boys
but, bleached by moonlight, aircraft wreckage thrown
into an open grave for broken toys.

An Icarus has fallen from the sky.
Another and another fall, a rain
of torches must have fallen. This clear eye
records the waste, does not insist on pain.

Pity witheld is power; a reservoir
of weeping gathers, war–dammed in the brain.

BOULOGNE SANDS

by P. Wilson Steer, painted circa 1890

Each holiday, the sea's withdrawing room
became a brief Atlantis. Here, through art,
a coloured mirage shimmers in its frame.
Girls, disciplined by clothes – in light straw hats,
black stockings, muslin dresses – dig the sand
and build small tumuli. Bright bathing-tents
conceal their changing bodies, while the wind
whitens the dark-blue waves that cunning paint
arrests and holds; so woven brushmarks fix
lost innocence on canvas, though high tide
chased all these children back to their hotels
a century ago. It scrubbed their works
from what proved to be minefields; here men died
where, long since, Granny built sand-citadels.

NEAR MAS DE LA DAME

Between the green and drunken vines
and silver-grey leaved olive groves,
I walked uphill along a sunbaked track,
looking for a remembered place:
a sunken lane that seemed, last time I came,
to be a bit of England in Provence.
As I approached the corner of that lane
I touched the shallows of a pool of shadow
spread by a forking cypress tree
that grew set back a little from the road.
It wasn't a dark pillar, like the others,
but slant and branchy, making a great roof,
and in its shelter, at a weathered table,
a woman sat and wrote.
    I said 'Bonjour Madame' as she looked up,
and she returned my greeting. I walked by
and found the hidden lane where noonday sun –
glaring through foliage – lit swallowtails
and yellow thistles while the loud cicadas
filed at high cypress bars. It was not England.
It wasn't even cooler than elsewhere.
As I returned, the lady still sat writing
at her ramshackle table in the shade,
like a recording angel, but no spirit;
not allegorical but personal.
    She wore real clothes, not robes: a cotton dress
and, covering grey hair, a light brown scarf
was knotted at her nape. Her bare brown arms
were strong as mine. Her sandals were like mine.
She kept her papers in old cardboard files:
she had no scrolls of parchment, no quill pen,
and, as I passed, her eyes met mine and smiled.
I would have liked to speak, but dared not do so.
What language to begin in? She looked English.
Was she writing a novel? Children's stories?
A treatise on cicadas? Marking devoirs
or working out her income-tax return?
Was she a poet who would keep the world
by power of praise from those who play with fire?

'See this,' she writes, 'and this. Such things are sacred.'
    I would have liked to ask, but dared not speak.
I didn't want to stop her flow of thought,
if she was thinking, or, if she was dreaming,
I didn't wish to wake her, or myself
if I was dreaming a projected self
who sits and writes under a fragrant cypress,
whatever else I may appear to do.
I didn't wish to learn she was a stranger
writing her private letters, not my wise
and ancient muse whose smiling silence blessed me.

A RIVER

Mere water, muttering over inanimate stones,
hemmed between hills and slowly eroded banks
bound by the cordon of trees it undermines,

is nothing a man cannot dam or divert, so he thinks.
Mere water, muttering meaningless syllables,
taking the line of least resistance, slinks

passively downstream, making its road of pebbles
as men made roads by following ambling cattle
between the readymade mountains' limestone tables.

But shallow and muttering water glitters like metal,
knowing itself the cutting-edge of a vast
landscape-carving machine whose work proves fatal

to mountain and valley alike. Millennia past,
its glacier grandfather gouged wide Ribblesdale out
from an exalted plateau of plankton-dust.

These drumlins are glacier-droppings. When thawed out
the ice left a cobbled valley of leaking lakes
that dwindled down to this river that mutters about

the Master of the Cloud-and-Ocean Works
who writes his name in water, so the river
bears the imprimatur that mankind lacks

and prints his changing signature forever.

THE CONSECRATION OF THE HOUSE

Light, clockwise, at the speed of time,
pans round and makes a time machine
of the synthetic cave dead hands
stacked up to shelter fodder, beast and hind.

Spearshafts of sunlight pierce our rooms;
midwinter noons project bright screens
on whitewashed walls, and bloodshot eyes
of sunsets stare us blind.

Iceblocks of bluish moonlight, stained
by violet snow beyond the sphere
of firelight, tell us, blizzard-bound,
the time when starved hare-shadows gnaw the ground.

This hollow sundial's second hand
wavers, but its inconstancy
has method in it. Sun and moonlight hands
lever this heavyweight, this rooted mound

of stones and all its freight through time:
creating days and months and years
that bear it through the centuries.
Our home's forgotten builders planned

its piercings well. Midwinter sun
shines clear through low-silled windows, but in June
the shadow-mottled light is almost drowned
by layered foliage and frond

and falls in watery patterns where –
some afternoon – the sun's flat footprints hint
that Someone called while passing, found
us out, but left the greeting of a friend.

Light consecrates the house, like love
and time. Here my grown children learned
to walk, and went away. Like sand
dust trickles through this year-glass. Suns wheel round

and pour their photons through my eyes.
Through twenty years of days and nights I've scanned
time's heliographs. Now I respond in kind
with happiness, brief radiance of mind.

A MEDITATION ON SOME DRAWINGS
OF DANDELION SEED-HEADS

Over ten years ago I made these marks –
brain-shadows of recurring shapes
that reappear each year, though light wind strips
scarred bases of the anchored rocket-ships
and carries seed far from the parent stalk
to settle on new sites and germinate.
They should have multiplied to numberless
brassyfaced weeds whose origin was here
in this ancestral spheroid's fluffy hair.
This was the worn-out and abandoned world
ten generations, scattered far afield,
have quite forgotten that they left behind.

I made these marks in Summer, sixty-nine.
My mother stayed with us. Our living-room
contained my sons and the demanding screen
that barters shadows for our time, and her
transfixed by spacemen walking on the moon.
I turned my back, but Granny and the boys
gawped at expensive hardware and stuffed guys
while I made drawings of an earthbound weed
whose astronauts know annual success
probing the wastes. But did my mother guess
her own inevitable, commonplace
yet awful journey into space drew near?

The seventies, on which we close the door,
were not for her. My first quite parentless
orphaned decade has whitened my brown hair,
so I resemble, in more ways than one,
those dandelions. Blown about a world
or universe of universities
my two young shock-heads seek a rooting bed
while my head ripens possibilities
of potent, breathborne seed, from inner space
where time stands still, though nearer, by ten years,
are our own journeys to untrodden stars
and the obituaries we may not read.

A BURIAL AT HORTON

The last of our adopted fathers, now –
on this green-island day, amid wild snows –
after an absence has come back for good
to lay his big, slow-moving farmer's bones
in Horton churchyard where schoolfellows lie
under the disappearing local names:
   Bill Redmayne, Mason Baines, Beck Heseltine.

You started up at Dub Cote, with one horse,
then marvelled that you owned the Squire's old house
and worked a double farm. Hard work did well,
but you're set in the past now, with the Squire,
and lines of men with rakes to turn green swathes
to hay, and Mary Ellen bringing tea,
   and all the fragrant grass of eighty years.

When we first came, your son was newly wed;
then, hand in hand, over the emerald ground,
he and his bride walked out to tend the lambs.
Now my first son, then crying like a lamb,
is grown through more than twenty lambing-times
and gone away, leaving his ghost behind
   with this year's children fishing in the beck.

The snowdrifts underline the drystone walls.
Olympian plaster mountains stare, aloof,
over green drumlin hills where you're at home:
where 'more snow comes to fetch old drifts away'
and 'it's two topcoats colder on the fells'
and 'never right warm when yon mountain's white,'
   and you were born, and knew thy way about.

You gave their first pay-packets to my boys
one haytime, and you said they worked like men.
Were they about sixteen? They came home late
on Summer nights bright with the haytime moon,
blind-drunk on work, and milk dipped from the churn,
and supper on the newly-shaven ground,
   smelling of sweat and hayseeds, oil, machines.

Those lads are in the past now, with the men
of the old village, who were lads with you
in this green hammock slung from those white peaks,
and children playing games along 'the Flat'
before the lorries commandeered all roads
such as the winding, one-way, switchback track
   that brought us here and will not take us back.

Your Sabbath-keeping used to rest the horse,
but tractors broke the custom. Breaking down,
machines keep random sabbaths of their own.
You mastered barns full of the new machines
but change from hay to silage finished you,
moving your landmarks round while you stood by.
   A full-time Sabbath claimed you in the end.

Stealing your cautious smile and careful thought
out of our sight and into history,
the plodding pace of one who walks all day
and never hurries, brought you to this place
where you are folded in, under the turf
spread with snow-fleeces, like a shearing ground,
   beside your wife, among the village names.

Bill Redmayne: Mason Baines: Beck Heseltine:
Jack Lambert, John, Meg in her haytime hat:
John Dinsdale, Dinsdale daughters, let Bob in.
The village of his boyhood swings its gate.
The grave heals first with snow, and then with grass:
then with forgetfulness. New villagers
   we shuffle up towards the empty place.

OLD EARTH REPUDIATES NEW SPRING

Flowers are not budding under my skin.
I wrap old Autumns about me – torn raincoats of leaves –
to hide this absurd petal-plumage. It's none of mine.
Above me the rooks draw level and regular graphs
across grey sky, thus proving all normal for March.
Perhaps the spinney's topmost boughs need oil;
small squeaky birds, migrating in restless flocks,
cling, high up, with feet like prehensile twigs.
The treecreeper's steep, erratic chart of his climb
up spindly trunks, and swift oblique flight down,
records no abnormal fever. Unheard tree-hearts
pump sapwood green with health. The pulse of the beck
where, passively, water ticks steadily out of the moss,
is calm. No white spate thunders.
Those twisted thorns are anemographs of spent gales;
their dryads are bent old women
and no god moans with desire in their arms any more.
And yet I cannot pretend these petals are snow,
though fieldfare flocks still feed on muckspread fields.
A clockwork wagtail moves among dung-caked cows,
newly evicted from shippons, with staggering calves
that must have tasted the Spring's illicit still,
like the drunk and disorderly lapwings. But I have not.
Clear cold water seeps through my mossy veins.
I have seen too many winters to be deceived.
The sycamore carries too many green birthday flames,
but the black-tipped ash betrays no joy. Nor I –
though codpiece buds may burst on red stemmed sallows.
At each twig-end green mercury breaks the glass.
I am nurse to a lovesick nature, untouched myself,
all antibody, immunised time after time;
my response to lovesongs is rook-raucous scorn.
(These petals are coincidental.) Hardbitten, twice shy
to expose any impulse again to the merciless sky,
I snatch my dun overall closer, to hide
sap-veined and bride-white flowers, but it has frayed
to silky fringes of luminous green
as vivid as I would be drab. How could I know –
when the south wind blew and the sun shone out of the cloud –

30

that so little kindness could warm and transform me, persuade
my case-hardened crust to soften and reveal
these sun-reflecting eyes, these trembling tongues,
this shameless calyx of scarlet and gold. I bloom
from frosted lips, and love in my own name.

MUTE MILTONS

1. *Solomon's Seal*

Mute Miltons have their moments. 'Buttercup,'
said one; 'Day's Eye', 'Earth Smoke', (the Fumitory);
One said 'Forget-me-not' and then shut up
his shop that coined small trademarks for wild goods
and lay down in a grave unmarked 'Anon'.
One first said 'Snowdrop,' now like snow he's gone.
Another found a lily in the woods
and watched bees baffled by its waxen beads
of sweetness, hung beneath a green leaf shield –
one of a curving stepladder that leant
on nothing – and these virgins-in-a-tent
were wives for Solomon whose rod unsealed
the maidenheads of twice ten-thousand brides.

2. *Dandelion*

Mute Miltons never wrote their scraps of song;
consenting ears adopted, memorised
those metaphors that leapt from tongue to tongue:
'Snapdragon', 'Bird's Eye', 'Foxglove'. Neighbours seized
upon such one-word poems. 'Lion's Tooth'
or 'Dent-de-Lion', inspired by ragged crowns
of torn and jagged lettuce, brought to birth
their name for wayside suns with yellow manes.
Old-wife-witchdoctors, knowing what they knew,
said 'Robin-pissabed,' (its milky blood
is diuretic); literally true
prose was forgotten, poetry preferred.
So 'Dandy Lion' won the people's vote,
with 'Primrose', 'Milkmaid', 'Mare's-tail', learnt by heart.

3. *Arum Maculatum, and others*

His poems, without benefit of print,
were breathed abroad like dandelion seeds.
He found them under hedges: 'Cuckoo Pint',
'Jack-in-the-Pulpit', then considered 'Lords
and Ladies', at their lovemaking, maybe;
(this plant makes a rude diagram to show
the principle of sex), but peasantry
in still-unravished England chose to see
Our Lady lap our Lord in her Green Shawl.
He meant no ribaldry, but bowed to look
Earth in her petalled eyes that moved his soul
to similes. He could have filled a book
with 'Ragged Robin', 'Eyebright', 'Cuckoospit':
his uncollected crops of wasteland wit.

SEPTEMBER, WITH GRASS-OF-PARNASSUS FLOWERS

Raddled and blowsy, fruitladen hat askew,
Ceres no longer cares for appearances;
her gait is a little unsteady, but she has come through

Summer's enormous task. Her abundances –
crocheted cell by cell from the mineral earth
and sunlight – are all but completed, so Ceres dances

homeward to sleep it off. Since Spring's first milktooth
snowdrop, she's been on call for unfolding, in situ,
buds within buds, birds, bugs; as ubiquitous midwife

delivering Summer's goods. Now, solid as statues,
masses of leathery leaves model trees into weighty
monuments to inventive and fecund virtue.

The windless air is an overpopulous city,
dusty with hoverers, hoovered forever by swallows.
Surplus lapwings and jackdaws eddy like litter.

Ceres can't go a step further; complacent and mellow,
she sits in a hedge, overdressed in scarlet beads,
smiling at gypsy ragwort's tarnishing yellow,

laughing at disarray of her carnival weeds.
Rosebay willowherb's last pink steeplejack petals
wave from their leaning spires in a blizzard of seeds.

Emptied, and thereby fulfilled, the goddess settles
down for a doze, drops off and begins to snore,
happy to die in this ditch among knapweed and nettles,

renouncing Olympus and the repeated chore
of turning stones into bread. She just can't face
decking old Earth in eternal youth once more.

Spiders veil the sleeping old woman in lace;
mists creep down from the mountains and spirit her bones
away, beyond vanished horizons, and leave in her place

sacred albino buttercups, signed with green veins.

VIEWS FROM THE ROAD

Cornfields lie toasting, poppies wave
    red handkerchiefs, our speed
    tosses the roadside weeds;
the hedgerow holds its flagdays, we might give
spare minutes that could change these paper favours
    to live, seedbearing roses, but the road –
                  the road will not release us.

Leaves dance on light, place flat green feet
    in patterns on the sky;
    trees overarch our way –
play oranges and lemons – this green throat
would swallow us forever, but its threat
    is shattered by the light, and still the road –
                  the road will not release us.

High intake meadows, combed and groomed
    by tractors, shine on fells;
    their Summer's stripped and baled,
so pale trapezoid kites, on sombre ground,
pattern the shadow-patterned hills. Backend
    camps cattle-tribes on aftergrass, but still
                  the road will not release us.

High-flying over little towns,
    swifts wheel like shooting bows
    and arrows after flies;
the question-mark of the young August moon
remains unanswered. Early she goes home
    before the night, before true darkness comes
                  the road will not release us.

WASPS' NEST

Beneath our lintel hung a papery breast
nippled with penetrating dark that pierced
the layered curtain of the Queen Wasp's nest.

Out of this summer palace, princelings flew;
some hunted, some had building work to do;
the population and the palace grew.

They fetched new wood-pulp, added paper ridges,
and, working backwards along selvages,
turbanned the nest in mummy-bandages.

A cabbage with grey leaves, drilled by a worm:
a pendent dome: a tumour on the beam:
a paper brain that hummed with thoughts of home:

the prison-chapel of a pregnant nun
who crouched in prayer, walled up from the sun,
to bear her thousand children one by one.

Her nursery, inverted tree of pods,
has hatched its hundreds, but the Queen still adds
more eggs, possessed by Summer's dying gods.

The princes' number dwindles. Still tight-laced
and elegant as ever – isthmus waist
links tiger-bustle to her pigeon-chest –

the venerable Queen within the walls
sits brooding over trays of cradle-cells
where perfect wasps lie dead beneath their seals.

A secret monument to Summer past,
she desiccates in darkness, grey with dust,
killed by the silent treachery of frost.

TORTOISESHELLS OVERWINTERING

In my bedroom ceiling's shadiest corner
   a dark encampment of inverted tents
is sitting out the tyranny of Winter.

Like Israelites that keep God's covenants
   in sober arks, or nomad Bedouins
who hide rich mats in fustian tenements,

they fold the magic carpets of their wings,
   concealing hieroglyphics of the meadow
clapped between tatter-bordered coverings.

As dingy as the withered nettlebed,
   as drab as marbled bibles, charred by fire,
or chips of bark or stone, they could be dead

but hang by wiry legs, as fine as hair,
   close-clustered near the plaster desert's edge
like a proscribed religious sect at prayer.

This bivouac preserves the Summer's page
   during eclipse of dandelions and daisies;
it bears pressed sparks of sun through this dark age:

one night between oasis and oasis.

IN THE IVORY TOWER

Voices of secretaries, porters, cleaners,
float up the echoing stairwell, into this attic
under the skylit roof in the southeast corner
of the Academy's edifice, where I sit writing.

Having no recognised function in this set-up,
being mere passenger, prisoner, parasite even,
I am the spy at its keyhole, the sounding stairwell
seems to be part of my ear, its spiral vortex

draws the chatter of cleaners, grumble of porters,
sonorous murmur of rumour, accents of power,
rustle of history's pages, whisper of dustfall,
sighs of futility, into my cerebral cortex.

I am the bug concealed behind the old master.
Amplifying its secrets, my pattering stairwell
acts as a gigantic deaf-aid and brings me the footfall
of Time's felt slippers on matted dust, their shuffle

whispers beneath the voices that, under the flagstones,
antique gods are rubble in dark foundations,
forgetting the hands that made them, forgetting the light,
forgetting the charges of joy and fear that begot them.

Yet ancient myths still haunt the working brain
this building resembles, although its inhabited cells
rattle with typists, intrays, teatrays, agenda,
balancing input and output and making art pay

wages to all its workers but not to me,
their innocent mole at large with a master key,
or eavesdropping spider spinning elastic lines
in keeping odd minutes in secret: a stowaway poet.

HEBRIDEAN SABBATH

Painted with rust, or grey as sea,
one-storey, corrugated-tin shacks stay
quiet as limpets at low tide, all day.

The Sabbath closes doors and hushes speech,
manacles hands, gyves feet, suppresses each
workaday wish for play, deserts the beach,

while people from the seashore houses wear
their Sundaybest expressions, oil their hair,
and walk in polished boots to meet for prayer.

Morning till evening, in swept living rooms
of every silent house, they welcome home
the One who made the world, and honour Him.

So, through the week, He, with them in the boats,
pulls in the fish, and grows green crests of oats
in hillside lazybeds. Where far bright floats

mark lobster kreels, He lures the prizes in;
always aware of Him, he cares for them,
even in cockleshells tossed by the storm.

And, from steep islands, women frequently
see God out walking on the wrinkled sea,
or, on high ledges where they scythe the hay

He runs in eddies, like a child at play,
on flower-carpets where the hailstones lay.

ANALYSIS OF THE SILENCE

This silence is lack of telephone-bells and traffic,
absence of feet through grass or keels through waves,
the gagging of rumour, or radio-voice and static,

and presence of shrill wren-signals, gannet-dives –
their splash, emergence, wing-claps of self-applause –
and sighs of pale, bottle-glass green sea that heaves

its sandbank mattress over: small motors of bees
that hum low over the ground: furtive crumble of walls,
and secret mitosis of cells in leaves: far cries

of squealing terns, discordant as unoiled wheels
above the deafening roar in the hub of the world's
invisible dynamo thundering here, that feels

like silence. But here, where deft gannets pin chiffon folds
of water scarves, I can hear, under all, the terrific
engines. Here is the axle-tree that holds

the planet in place, and controls the unsleeping traffic.

BLACK-HOUSE WOMAN

I am, myself, the house that shelters them.
My nerves extend into this skirt of stone,
this shawl of thatch. These windows are my eyes.
I am a hollow room, enfolding men.

The peat fire is my heart. This hearth is warm
always, for them, but through the open door
sometimes shy happiness steals in to me.
The sun lays yellow carpets on the floor.

My children bring home hunger, men bring storm,
and I absorb in quiet the sea-bird's cry,
the breakers' roar, till in the sleeping room
oceans and mountains lie.

They leave no room for me in my own womb;
by them, and by their dreams, my lap is filled;
I spread my skirts to shield them, I am home,
content to be my one forgotten child.

WHAT'S DONE CANNOT BE UNDONE

The tide crawls forward now
washing the beach more thoroughly
than might seem necessary.
One wave, I think, would be enough;
but, obsessed, the scrubbing arm
sweeps round wide arcs of foam.
Returning water files through crevices
and shakes out weed to lay it slanting seaward.
It polishes, repeatedly, meticulously dries
already spotless sand. You might think it erased
an army's footprints, or deodorised
the bed of a mass orgy.
But almost no one has been here.
A gull or two flew down and stood about;
a chain of three-toed tracks
wavers along the shore.
Last night an otter scurried round the rocks
and ran into the sea.
Perhaps a few small necessary murders –
such as maintain the world – have taken place:
nothing that warrants this
fanatical twice-daily cleanliness
of waves destroying evidence of guilt
but not the spot itself. And waves forget
that they have washed all proof away.
Only their own faint overlapping tracks,
like tiles laid upside-down, remain.
So, tirelessly, the tide begins again.
Last Winter, not remarkable for storms,
it scoured a beach of sand away.
The sea lathers my feet. As I step back,
it sets to work on my few idle marks.

SCARP SONG

My two strong sons skate out in one small shoe
                treading the polished water
across inverted hills that hang stone heads
among the white clouds in its green glass mirror.

The wind sleeps, and a blanket mist may thicken,
                hiding the polished water,
and no one knows which breathing wind may cloud
the glass, and frost or shiver the green mirror.

All my love's work sits in that far white boat,
                trusting the smiling traitor,
diminishes beyond duststorms of birds.
I see long threads of white hair in the mirror.

My sons ride fearlessly, far out to sea;
                I would not have them other:
they cheat the traitor of his mackerel shoal
and teach the lobster to repent his error.

Northeaster, chase them home; bring rainbow weather
                across the ruffled water.
Confine, Southwest, remorseless water-walls
that travel blind. I dare not name my terror.

OTTER LETTER

I knew you at first glance, though far offshore,
disporting in the satin-surfaced sea.
You were no seal – too small, and too alert –
you hadn't that forsaken-merman stare
with which seals look at land, as though a man
were bedded in that seamless blubber coat.
You hadn't their blunt, slablike look, but peered
inquisitively, with your pointed head
craning from feline shoulders, at the brash
and shouting perpendiculars that walked.
You looked amazed – amused –
at our impedimenta – rubber boats,
our oars and engines – where, just in your skin,
you're fearlessly, amphibiously, at home
and, I suspect, glad not to be a man.
You own the title deeds to rocks and caves:
you've signed the parchment beach. Your tracks confirm
possession. Here you landed, shook yourself
and scratched up sand, and rolled, then wrote along
the lines between obliterating waves
and last saliva splash of lapping tide.
This is an otter beach. Your kind belongs
to seas where we are poor forked aliens –
helpless without those cities at our backs
that make our adaptations to your world.
Insouciant as a cormorant, you dived –
I glimpsed your flank, which curved like a small wave –
and disappeared into your element.
Since then your streamlined joy possesses me,
and leads me on to write.
For all our lacks –
our insulating boots and plastic macs,
sea crutches, sea-bathchairs, and our false limbs –
we human have some assets. Empathy.
We dive into mind's all-reflecting sea
for images, and words that leave live tracks.

DEPOPULATION PLAY, SET ON THE ISLAND OF SCARP, WITH A CAST OF NO ONE

The scenery is well enough,
but what about the actors? What indeed?
The heroine grew old,
remembered everything except her lines
and died. The heroes left –
renouncing crowns and titles – long ago,
and went to Glasgow. Only clowns remained
to play to empty houses:
houses once full of laughter, silent now,
or full of scornful birds.
Exits were made in weeping groups, by boat,
not drawn by swans but driven by machines
leaving an oily wake, to no applause.
And no one volunteered for Crusoe's part
except for amateurs, who soon gave up
after a few brief seasons, but –
compelled – the show goes on.
Gauzes drift in, mad as Ophelia,
uncertain of their cues, and then dissolve.
The safety curtain falls and sticks half-way,
blots out the stage while scene-shifters wheel in
the same old rocks and mountains, then
rainbows and storms, lost properties,
a lobster-boat from a far-distant play,
some ship of fools, opposing winds,
alarums and excursions, silences.
A squall sets waves to smiling false white smiles;
the beach is strewn with wigs
and litter hurled ashore by hissing seas.
The script is wordless, may be meaningless,
by poltergeists, or by the Lighting Man.
The drama is of light. Topping the bill
are tightrope-walking Sun, Trapezing Moon.
The sea itself changes its coloured lights,
gives Winter matinees, and plays all night
to choruses of stars.

THE ISLAND TAX

for David Fry

His Majesty the Sea demands –
    every decade or so – an Island Tax,
and snatches children from the sands
    or fishermen from rocks;
        just when we least expect it
        he takes a boat and wrecks it.

Between implacable demands
    his hushing lulls us almost into sleep.
The Sea Lord feeds us, condescends
    to lend the roof across his deep
        as playground and provider;
        his minions fill our larder.

He salivates around our shores
    and undermines the cliff from which I hear
his waves in sea-caves, slamming doors
    on grumbling Minotaur:
        someone must pay protection
        to our great neighbour's faction.

The papery tufts of Sea-pink shake;
    the sea-skin shudders and a sail lies down;
in waters quiet as a lake
    unwary swimmers drown;
        out in those wide blue spaces
        assassins leave no traces.

The King conscripts his forces
    commanded by a gale-force Southwest wind;
long ranks of white-plumed horses
    advance against the land:
        but that's an ancient story,
        my tale's contemporary.

The Mafioso Sea has sent
    his tall green debt-collector to our door
to execute an innocent
    whom we shall see no more.
        Swifter than cobras, breakers
        rush over rocks to take us.

TIME'S AMBUSH

1

Encyclopaedia Britannica,
Fourteenth edition, nineteen-twenty-nine,
arrived when I was four. Its packing-case
was made into a dolls' house; that was mine.
The books were for our father's use.

A to Anno, Annus, Balt to Brai.

Green volumes, heavy with profundities
on flimsy India paper – Brai to Cast –
proved dull to read, and large for my small knees.
I liked the photographs of statues best:
old marble Greeks with marble penises.

Cast to Cole to Dama and Educ.

I should have read the small print, might have learned
to know beforehand what I knew too late.
Educ for Education might have warned –
Extr to Game – but prescience helps fate,
avoidance leads us to what lies in wait.

Gunn, Jere, Libe, Libi, Mary, Mus.

My sister Mary plucked the lotus Mus
for Music. Mus to Ozon, P to Plan:
I lacked a plan – Rayn Sarr – time's Sorcerers
concealed their Sordid Texts from both of us
through Text to Vasc, and still I could not guess

time's present hidden in the final one.

Atlas and Index. On the English map
of roads and towns and villages, a word
adorned a spot stuck to a railway line,
and near that village station a green road
led to a house predestined to be mine

for even then it bore my maiden name.

49

2

If, then, I could have used a magic lens
or been God's pupil, a creative eye,
so probed into the crevices of paper
and animated printed words and signs,
I would have seen this drumlinned valley, slung
between its limestone hills, on that flat map,
with farms linked by a skein of narrow lanes.

I would have seen those flyspecks on pale green,
those minute rectangles, as houses, barns
and scattered villages, inhabited
by map-mites that, when magnified, proved men
and horses, sheep and cattle, dogs and stones
and round-armed women, laid now with the dead,
running to save dry washing from the rain.

Late-lying bones beneath the quilted green
communal counterpane strode easily
upright along the lanes, or caught their horses,
harnessing them to carts to drive to town
on market-days, and some came tipsily
home to this house: but all past time took place
elsewhere in space. Creation spirals on

and brings me to this April among hills
much like the ones concealed in that old map
when it was new and folded among books
on our suburban shelves. Along stone walls,
snowdrifts define enclosures: Ulmber, Stripe,
Great Outiber and Thistle Bottom, Crooks
and Dunnyworth; all drawn with long white strokes.

Under a clouded moon the pale drifts gleam
luminous as clock-hands on the dial
of Ribblesdale: dish with a broken rim;
they signal change in cursive Arabic
or Greek. I read their cyphers in the dark,
sensing, underneath the diagram,
the wound-up spring of Spring, changing the clock.

UNRECORDED SPEECH

She says 'How was you?' Kissing. 'Come on in,
I'm all of a muck-sweat, having a merry-go-round;
you've caught me doing my work.'
She doesn't clean, but circumvents the dirt.
Chairs stand on tables – 'All of a tizz-wozz.'
(Has that been spelt before?) 'A lick of paint,'
she says, propping her brush in turps,
'freshens things up a bit.' She paints the door
and skirting boards; washes white window-veils.
Houses, bedsitters, flats, extend herself.
She makes the best of it, but likes a move;
it's like a change of dress, changing address.
I've lost count of the changes. 'Home at last!'
was said too often to be credible.
We'll write it on her tomb, or jar of ash,
unless she sees us out.
She says 'The poor old lady' of someone
no older than herself.
'She's gone a bit – you know dear – gone a bit
doo-lally. Poor old thing. It takes all sorts –'
From childhood she remembers sparkling frost,
and walking out in it in Christmas clothes –
a coat her mother made her – vivid mauve –
'so bright against the snow.'
'And of a Friday afternoon
the teacher read to us. That was the best.'
Stories have been essential food since then.
Peg's Paper, H. E. Bates, Hardy and all
except romances; 'that don't interest me.'
She fills her days 'somehow', since Hubby died,
but she has grown since then.
'All in a lifetime dear,' she says of death.
Her words may be dead language soon;
that's why I write them down. They will be heard
'never no more,' as she said at the birth
of my husband, her only child,
proving that double negatives mean 'No'.

from THE SPOKEN POEMS
OF ELIZABETH WINIFRED ROSE

1.   *Her Dancing Days, or the death of Mantovani set her off*

Those old tunes take me back. I used to go
to dances every Saturday. Of course
I wasn't never going to give it up,
and nor was Lily Cannon, but we did.
We wasn't taught, we just picked up the steps.
In Summer there was dances in Brent Park;
they called them 'flannel dances': out of doors.
The men could wear grey flannels, not the girls.
I used to make my dresses, buy the stuff
up Cricklewood, and sew them in a day.
I liked the winter evening dances best,
and used to dance with Horace – he was tall,
and we danced well together – Percival –
he was a butler, rather serious –
Jack Roach, Jack Young, and I forget who else:
but there was one I used to like, and then
one Saturday he wasn't there, and I
was heartbroke. Then he wrote.
I was to meet him at the Bald Faced Stag
one Sunday afternoon. We'd never met
by day. I didn't like the looks of him.
And Horace was engaged. Then, at a fair
with Lil, she was all out for a good time,
we met these two. One of them wore a cap.
I don't like caps. 'I'll have him then,' said Lil:
all four slid down the helter-skelter, then
the heel come off me shoe; I had to hop;
he fixed it for me. Later, we arranged
to meet again next evening at the Hyde.
    Lily come round, and sat down by the fire
to knit. 'I'm going out,' I said; 'You're not,
it's raining.' But I was. I had to go.
We didn't know each other's names,
or where we worked, or any thing.
And there he waited for me, in the wet,
and fifty years began.

I said I'd never give up dancing, and
he said the same of football, but we did;
and Lily gave up dancing too, quite soon.
    We was both seventeen.

BALLAD OF THE GOOD OLD DAYS

When Grandad was eleven
   he walked the winding lanes
from Hampshire up to London
   and found some work in Staines.

As bricklayer's apprentice,
   with three shillin a week –
which paid for food but not a bed –
   he slept free, in a rick.

But they was good old days, for we was young
and Nature danced us on her puppet-string.

He walked the London pavements
   as master of his trade,
and out to post a letter ran
   an apronned serving maid.

He walked the London pavements
   to seek for any work
to keep the wife that was that maid,
   but he found little luck.

But they was good old days, at your wits' end
you never knew what Providence might send.

At home with her two babies
   without a bit of bread
and not a penny in the house,
   poor Granny raised her head;

She heard the front-door rattle,
   she heard a letter fall,
and found, inside it, half-a-crown
   and no one's name at all.

So they was good old days, for we was fed,
and Someone watched us, else we would be dead.

Then, in a darkened London
    the Good Times came around,
and, working in munitions,
    prosperity was found.

Now there was work for Grandad
    and Granny's heart had ease;
blood-money came in regular,
    unlike the pay of peace.

But they was good old days, them years gone by,
before old Nature dropped us where we lie.

from SOHO SONGS

What has become of Rose?
She came to town with neither As nor Os
to sell her assets fresh; solicitin'.

With bloodied apron, like a randy ram
reddled to mark the ewes, the butcher stands
by his refrigerated marble slab
and offers chopped-up bodies, flesh
of innocents, small shoulders, legs of lamb,
cutlets of newborn babe, bled white
and skilfully disjointed. Small pink piglets'
high-heeled trotters patter home no more
along the midnight gutters. Tasty giblets,
chicken-skinned white thighs and tender calves,
spare-ribs, plump rumps, trays of small testicles
in breadcrumbs, and mature sheep's rolling eyes.
Eviscerated torsos swing from hooks
in Bluebeard's coldstore, and along these racks
hang well dressed game birds, elegant, unruffled
but bleeding from the beak, and fluffy bunnies
hang with their running noses rammed in buckets.
Dismembered chicks – legs, wings and breasts –
are strewn like bombers' victims. Broken hearts
and thoughtless brains, meatpies and sausages:
and no one knows what's in them; no one knows

what has become of Rose
who came to town with neither As nor Os,
solicitin'.

EPISTLE TO THE MAN WHO SLEEPS
IN SHERWOOD STREET

I thought you were a dead man, more than once,
as you lay on the paving-stones
of Sherwood Street, West One. That first cold spell
of our first Winter here, you used to lie
under an overhang that kept you dry
but nothing, no amount of newspaper,
could keep you warm enough to keep alive.
But you had found a vent from underground
and seldom left your pitch, but entertained
strange friends to bottled breakfast, any time.
    In Spring you disappeared.
Your paving-stones fell vacant, and remained so.
All through high Summer silky brownskinned legs
no longer made fastidious diversions
into the gutter, or crossed Sherwood Street
in order to pass by at a safe distance.
I thought you had moved house into the park
but when November came you were not back
so then I thought you must have gone away
for good, dressed in a plastic sack;
And he's well out of it, I thought.
    Yet, several times, I saw your lookalike
sleeping, defenceless, on a seat, but he
was younger, older, beardless, fatter, thinner;
one had a swollen eye, closed up with bruises;
I saw one zigzagging across the traffic
and gibbering at his shadow in a window,
.but the reflection was a total stranger,
though not teetotal. And one like you slept
sound on a marble mattress, the broad step
of vacant premises by Upper John Street.
He might have been your brother, but was not
your very self, the one your mother loved
enough to rear you through man's chancy childhood.
    Then one fine day last week I saw –
with a surprising joy – in Sherwood Street,
on a low scaffold plank, you, fast asleep:
leathery-skinned and bearded, dirty, mad
and laughing in your grand fourposter bed.

LULLABY FOR A MAN ASLEEP
IN BREWER STREET

I wish you sweeter dreams
   than you can buy in Soho
from Kinky Madam Jo-Jo
   at Adults Only Peepshow.

I wish you more convincing
   and better, more entrancing
visions than Real Naked Girls
   all Nonstop Go-Go Dancing.

I wish the Double Bedshow,
   the Rentaboy Arcade,
the Fully Frontal Sideshow,
   were plunged into the shade

by an authentic Heaven
   which each unfolding rose
in Golden Square announces,
   where Second Childhood goes.

I wish the marble doorstep
   whereon you take your nap
would soften, and you waken
   in your lost mother's lap

with all your nightmares broken,
   and bloodshot eyes, grown bright,
see shameless angels dancing
   like dustmotes in the light.

PRAMPUSHERS

We have been shunted to a quiet siding:
the streamlined express-trains, with lovers riding
off on excursions to the continent,
go whooping by, while we must be content
with clanking up and down past cinder-mounds
and all the furniture of no-man's-lands –
coal mountains, coke-stacks, cylinders for gas,
(instead of Paris, Venice, Alpine pass),
where old allotments, past the engine sheds,
grow willowherb plantations, nettlebeds.
No longer oriental express dragons,
we loiter here like pensioned cattle-wagons,
among the most peripheral affairs
in nature's citadel of nursing-chairs.

That railway siding was a mere conceit.
I must be truthful, not exaggerate.
Nevertheless, though long since put away,
the things appropriate to childhood's day
have to be taken back. The mind grows dark
and, exiled to the desert of the park,
we push the prams beneath the weeping tree,
concealing crises of identity.

We push the swings, and laugh as gaily as
the other mothers, watched by dahlias,
and sigh among the shrubberies, alone.
The dead-leaf bonfire smoke comes drifting down
the terraced gardens. Mazes of clipped privet
reprove us. Blow your nose. Think nothing of it:
but there's still someone sobbing in the garden,
ungrateful for this imitation Eden
where nightingales have long been out of season
but cabbage roses bloom and bloom. What reason
can there be here for grief? The spider weaves
lace curtains. Trees lay carpets of red leaves.
Come, push your pram; on artificial lakes
flotillas of uncomplicated ducks
are laughing. Why, among the laurel trees,

do you still weep? Municipalities
provide secluded benches for your ease.
Sit on our wooden laps, dry foolish eyes
that cannot recognise true happiness.

What inner desolation, what distress,
what serpent spoils the council's barbered grass?
You may not weep for married loneliness.

GREEN RESISTANCE

Dark walls press close and closer round
the Keeper's so-called garden, sun-deprived
neglected gryke of ground
between Academy and Albany
where plants are photon-starved.

Green gardens reached to Soho once,
when Swift and Johnson lived,
but London outstripped nature, grew more dense
till, in a well of shadow, clipped between
brick precipices, only this survived.

A locked sub-station, full of shocking switches,
stands hard on much of it;
through sooty walls each office window watches,
and from high stacks the chimney-pigeons spy
into the dungeon-pit.

Under such pressure as this remnant bears,
oppressed by alien Knotweed, (prison guards
that pierce the flags with forests of red spears),
earth must rebel or die, so I enrol
myself in this green cell.

ORION IN SEPTEMBER:
A JOURNEY HOME

Above the car park, bright as diamonds,
Orion leaping in the southern dark
from midnight to extinction in the sun
was my last souvenir, found as we left
one hour before the dawn.

We drove out of the Midi: crossed the Rhône
and crawled by hairpin bends to that high plain
where, white as marble statues on the green,
calm tribes of cattle graze. They sit or stand
like warm and breathing stone.

Still carrying my gift, Orion's brooch,
inside my head, I came to Vézelay
where on his tympanum, high out of reach,
a Christ in Glory spreads out giant hands
to give his light away.

A supernatural wind blows through the stone
and animates the saints; their draperies
are dancing though their limbs are sitting down,
and like a sea alive with vortices
is Lord Jesus's gown.

I think of those tumultuous night skies
that Vincent caught in whirlpools of blue marks.
He longed to reach the stars. His piercing eyes
saw them as more than matter, or mere sparks,
but heavenly destinies

though he did not believe. Awestruck Anon,
eight hundred years before, gazing by night,
saw that vast firefly dance. Between each one
he joined the dots to make a Man of Light
who heard the prayers of men.

Stars answer eyes and eyes reflect the stars;
a great Sky Father swings across the deep
reflected in our minds. His bright trapeze –
Orion's belted quadrilateral –
glitters throughout our sleep.

THREE WOMEN WHO LIVE IN ART:
A TRIPTYCH

I.   *Gislebert's* Eve, *in Autun, Burgundy*

Snake is implicit in the tree;
    its ringstraked branches curve like ropes
to proffer Eve ripe apples, free.

Her seed sleeps, hidden, like the pips
    in clustered grapes on coiling vines
that spread their fan to veil her hips.

Snake slides between the chiselled lines –
    combed parallel – of wavy hair,
and undulates, as Eve reclines,

in limbs that swim for Time's fresh air
    out of Eternity's arrest.
She cannot live as pure Idea.

I see a schoolgirl's nubile breast
    and greedy profile; know her eye
lacks innocence, is filled with lust

to pierce the skin of latency.

2.   Mother with Two Children *by Egon Schiele*

My fruit devours me, drinks me,
lives by my depletion;
these are my rosy apples,
my painted clowns, my children
that brighten as I fade.

They rise out of my ashes
in multi-coloured plumage –
striped coats and vivid sashes
like pretty patchwork gypsies –
the dolls my body made

64

that sit on both my hands.
I am not free, not free
but bound and mute. Love thinks me
fulfilled: a laden tree.

3.   *A Duccio Madonna and Child*

for Pamela Izzard, and in memory of Polly

Mourning mother of a mortal god,
   the mannikin you weep for dries your tears
but still you weep, till your blue cloak and hood
   are dark as midnight with clairvoyant fears.
You have condemned an innocent to die.
   The mandatory price for drawing breath
is death by want, disease, time's atrophy
   or crucifixion; and you know this truth
too well, for – changing like Madonna Moon –
   you will yourself betray and undermine
and execute, then – laying out your son –
   will drain his blood and strip his skeleton.
Therefore you grieve, while offering with love
Earth's playground crazed with pathways to the grave.

WORM

This drizzle rots white tapes
of wallside snow, thaws out
the earth so that a worm escapes

to probe, with tapered snout,
hard tarmac where it cannot find –
although it gropes about –

the way back underground.
It stretches out its span
of pearl-complexioned, blind

and naked gut, grows thin
and long, and then contracts
its length again.

It seems the fool elects
to cross the rainwet road
while ignorant of facts

such as: it is thrush-food,
and there are tractor-wheels.
Misguided annelid,

you seem to have two tails
but one's your brainless head.
Unminded grit-canals

should hide beneath the mud:
why not move in reverse
and thus go back to bed

before your plight grows worse?
Its boneless finger points
across a universe

of road, so, all at once
I seize the creature's saddle.
Convulsed, and lacking joints,

it knots into a muddle
which I set down on grass.
Released from its tight huddle

it burrows. Soon its arse
waves me goodbye, withdraws
to worms' nutritious house:

the home of both of us.

TRAGOPOGON MINOR,
OR LESSER GOATSBEARD

i.m. Patrick Symons R.A.

This elegance of stem and fluted bud
    appears to promise something more than common:
    better than scruffy Hawkbit – something Roman –
purple as Caesar's toga – or the red
of roses, sunsets, blood.

But in the yawning involucre, a frill
of misfit yellow petals fails to fill
    its setting, seeming prematurely born,
    unfinished, and the vulgar Dandelion
outshines it. Is this all?

Not yet. It folds the disappointing rose
    at which the small flies fed, purses its bud
and clips its spent fires close. It undergoes
    gestation of its seed, appearing dead,
but its grey goat's beard grows

until a silo of live bombs unlocks
    this spheroid Chinese globe that spills white fire
from cobweb cups, this nest of shuttlecocks
    or spindles fletched with spider-silk: then air
lifts off furled promises by their white hair.

THE GREAT ANTEATER AND THE ANTS

Between the tapered neck and baton snout
its skull appears more of a swollen joint
than brainbox full of thought
    as the diagonally banded
    Great Anteater, hook handed,
quests eagerly about
obsessed by one idea, the crumb sized Ant
   which it consumes by millions to sustain
   its bulk and energy to pace the plain.

On the horizon of its dreams
stand Anthills full of nourishment;
its curved claws itch to rip their seams
    and open up dark tenements
    of innocents;
its toothless jaws unroll their ream
of tubular flypaper tongue
   to lick whole teams of workers from their toil
   then probe for further spoil.

It is a specialist: no other skill
dwells in its tiny brain.
It has no notions about pest-control,
    it bears Ant no illwill
    but has a gut to fill
so devastates the Cities of the Plain
as though it were God's Wrath or the Black Death.
   Then Ant, though thousands have been killed,
   gathers her scattered rubble to rebuild.

The Cataclysmic Beast withdraws,
digesting individual dooms;
it curls up in its den and snores –
    (under black horsehair blanket tails
    females look just like males) –
and suffers no remorse.
It is impersonal, and only seems
   to be a moral agent, sent to punish
   unlucky Ants who vanish.

DRAGONFLY CONSIDERS HELICOPTER

for Chris O'Toole

Some say the idol, Screw-Wing, is our god,
    but I am not fooled
and will not be fobbed off with mined and made
    toys of newfangled Man. We are too old.

Machines are forgeries that cannot think;
    with dreaming minds
we cling, rightangled, to the sedge, our link
    to half-forgotten ponds

where many times our wingless souls have lived.
    My fishbowl head
is like a diver's helmet. I have dived
    repeatedly, and been new-made from mud.

Sedge is our birth-cord from the watery bag
    into the summer skies;
resting from flight that flashed zigzag, zigzag,
    I praise our beauty, and my compound eyes

compare the noisy Screw-Wing overhead
    with us, the seminal thought
from slow Creation's carboniferous bed.
    A pseudo-insect's lifespan must be short.

We posture on the sedges like straight flags –
    we Devil's Darners –
clasping our rungless ladders with six legs
    of brittle chitin bent at flexy corners

so that our jewelled tails lie horizontal.
    Glass wings unfurled,
I hold my pose with pride in fundamental
    knowledge. I'm the linchpin of the world.

THE BLACKCAPS IN THE NEGLECTED
JEWISH CEMETERY IN VIENNA

For unknown motives – shame or civic pride
   or guilt, or tidiness – men saw and slash
the forest, moving like a ruinous tide.

They sever branches from slim boles of ash
   and sycamore; by felling poles they fold
a green tent canopied with leafy mesh.

Its complex density, its curtain walls
   accommodated nests in cavities
that hid bird-nurseries from crow patrols.

The reappearing monuments arise
   through the subsiding thicket, shoved awry
by roots and ivy's ropey arteries,

while, stacked in pyres, the naked saplings lie
   reminding us of bony body-mounds
as though the past had stained eternity

or burned our retinas. There's no amends
   for murdered innocents. Pogroms of trees
make matters worse. No safe house now defends

the warblers in yarmulkas. Refugees
   are on the move again. A small Jew-ghost –
the tiny cantor in his kuppel – flees

from desolation where he built his nest.

FOR THE SIX CHILDREN OF DR GOEBBELS

*'. . . their playing was halted and they were given lethal injec-
tions, apparently by the same physician who the day before had
poisoned the Fuehrer's dogs.'* (from *The Rise and Fall of the
Third Reich*, by William L. Shirer)

Mayday: mayday: what did you play
in Uncle Herod's bunker? Murder?
Happy families? or houses?
Richard Wagner's ring-o-roses?
Götterdämmerung or Ludo?
Bombs were raining from the skies;
Daddy's house was built of lies.

Hela, Hilda, Helmut, Holde,
Hedda, Heide, (Hitler's echoes),
did you play at snakes and ladders?
consequences? hide-and-seek?
or following, into the dark,
your Leader? And weren't you afraid
of Doctor Daddy's liebestod?

Did Holde have bad dreams, and cry
of Bolsheviks that hunt the wolfpack
to its lair, and kill them all –
even wolfcubs – hang them up
by the tails from crooked nails,
like Uncle Musso, by the heels,
like Hilda hanging Jewish dolls.

Hela, Hilda, Helmut, Holde,
Hedda, Heide: shadow puppets
cast by darkness, had to vanish
like six puffs of propaganda.
Innocent, by definition;
doomed, for Daddy's house of lies
was falling, and no wonder.

Mothers and fathers: Hansel and Gretel:
Who killed Cock Robin? Evil is good.
This is the gingerbread house in the wood.
Pity is weakness, so harden your heart:
I, said the Sparrow, I poisoned the dart.
Mother is sobbing, longing to die:
six more dead children in History Pie.

AT MAUTHAUSEN CAMP

If there is a god, he will have to beg me for forgiveness.
(Graffiti at Mauthausen Camp)

To use such sufferings
as raw material
for art, is not permitted;
and yet I wish to add
a token, like those flowers
on the Italians' wall.
I wish the dead could know
that we know how they died,
that we might touch their hands.
No monument can do it,
no bronze, no rusting iron,
nor formalised barbed wire,
nor Berthold Brecht quotations.
Perhaps this crown of thorns
with name-tags speared on each
pitiless spike, says something.
These photographs of faces
when they had flesh on them
express that they were loved
and individual
but cannot bring them back.
Perhaps they haunt the stairs –
these steep and broken stairs
that sweep down to the quarry
like a dry waterfall
that was a fall of men:
but they cannot return
to vulnerable sense
to be abused again,
and would not if they could.
It is our minds they haunt.
By climbing up those stairs
and resting only once
I made my offering.
What use was that? No use.
It proved that I am lucky
in living on past sixty.

I see the species–rich
meadow above mass graves
where Yugoslavs and Poles,
Hungarians and Jews,
Bulgarians and Danes,
Dutchmen and Frenchmen lie
by Germans and Italians.
I think: The Earth forgives.
Forgiveness is not just.
There can be no amends
except remembering
bloodfalls where starved men fell
beneath heartbreaking stones
and each was I – and I –
and I –

WATER REMEMBERS

for James Harpur

When frost draws fishbone and fern on windowpanes,
water is running through memories, tracing forms
like starry mosses, muscles and intricate brains.

                    Water has been there.

Thus as liverwort tongues it overlapped;
thus it feathered the coalmeasure forest fronds,
and thus it was combed by mermaidens' cold webbed hands.

                    Water remembers

bloody adventures as Man, and many deaths
from which it emerged unscathed, as from the fire
water ascends as a ghost and descends as a shower.

                    Water reminds us

nothing that truly exists can ever be lost.
It recapitulates its countless loves,
having been present at every winesodden wedding

                    and virgin's deflowering.

Water confetti falls on the winter forest,
loading all trees alike with spurious blossom,
heavy as fruit, that bends then breaks the branches.

                    Crutches of water

prop every plant in the forest. Making, unmaking,
water is omnipresent and taken for granted,
being, perhaps, mere ambassador, deputy, servant

                    of something forgotten.

MISTER JARMAN'S GHOSTS

Don't you find it creepy, Missis Adams?
I feel it on them stairs: a sort of coldness;
and you fly up and down quite quick, I notice.
I used to do the same myself, but now
old Annie Domino has slowed me down.
    I started here on night security,
and one night, after midnight, on that landing,
I met a lady. She was very small,
not five foot high, dressed in old-fashioned clothes.
She said 'Who are you? Tell me who you are.'
She had a small, high, strangled sort of voice:
old and far off. I didn't tell her nothing.
Then once, in the front hall, Sir Allan Grant
glided towards me through a haze of smoke.
That's how you tell it's them. They come through smoke,
and it's all dark behind them, spangled like
with Christmas glitter. He was like his bust.
And then, by day, I saw another lady.
I couldn't see her face but saw her dress
had lots of little buttons, glass, or diamonds.
She walked away with quick but tiny steps –
like this. An old chap told me I had seen
the woman who kept house when he was young.
'You got her to a tee,' he said. Quite often,
up in the Private Rooms, I seen a shadow.
It moves across the windows, and I've heard –
down by Nun's Walk – a scream like someone murdered.
Then someone set a tape-recorder up
outside the restaurant, and left it running,
recording all the noises of the night:
the pipes and groaning fridges, then this scream.
They got it on the tape: a woman screaming.
    One night, down in the vaults, one tapped my shoulder.
I turned, and there was no one. I'm a psychic.
The lady from the Psychical Research
said I was Extrasensitive. My Mother
would give what she could spare to those in trouble.
She was religious. I'm a seventh child.
That's why I got this gift. I see and hear them.
    Haven't you never seen one, Missis Adams?

FROM MRS ORPHEUS TO HER SON

Love, not music, let me through the gate –
the one-way turnstile to the Underworld
whose dreadful gravity tugged at my heart

and forced me to descend through tunnelled ground
into the land of shades where money failed –
although they say the password's 'cash-in-hand'.

Love let me through dim booking-halls, all filled
with demons in official caps and badges,
and rife with omens. Someone had been killed.

I fled the hubbub to the outer edges –
a basement in a suburb of this town
where you wrote messages on grubby pages:

although they made no sense you wrote them down,
thinking to crack a code in random words
dictated by the voice behind your frown.

'You cannot live in Hades with the dead:
escape with me. I think I know a way.'
Obediently you followed where I led

up the steep track towards the common day;
but as the darkness drained into the earth
your shadow took the heaviness of clay.

Just as one's body, weightless in the bath,
grows leaden climbing out, you could not haul
one limb after another up the path.

I could not pull you up but let you fall,
and so you sank into the murky air.
It takes a Hercules to drag from Hell

one soul. An aging woman cannot bear
her son again. My heart, grown like a stone,
was all that I could carry. The cave where

I lost you, you must struggle through alone.

SHOPPING LISTS

All pocket archaeologists
    digging for railcards, coins and keys,
find superseded shopping lists:
    torn shards of petty histories.

In shorthand jottings, all of life
    is hinted at on strips of scrap:
rye bread, red wine (all drunk), minced beef,
    pig-liver for the cat (now dead, poor chap).

Go to the bank: pay in, draw out;
    Greengrocer: beansprouts, fruit, courgettes;
Fish Barrow: mackerel or trout;
    a dozen eggs for omelettes.

Cornfields come with the brown bread rolls,
    orchards with apples, and the sea
heaves, vast, around the herring shoals,
    and China swims in Lapsang Souchong tea.

Wine glasses, green, recycled ones,
    potscourer, Persil, margarine –
implying fields of petalled suns,
    great crowds of holy fellahin.

Post Office, pension, porridge-oats;
    pay garage bill, buy *Radio Times* –
implying music, (storms of notes),
    and News of ghastly human crimes.

These cancelled litanies of stuff
    consumed, excreted, day by day,
can never say the word 'Enough'
    though they suggest futility,

but, join the dots, they sketch a place
    and time, with dreams that come and go,
now passed to endless outer space –
    digested days that nourish Now.

THE DRAINING OF THE LAKE

Across the lake's long waist, close to the bridge
that belts the Pall Mall to the Whitehall side,
workmen in waders build a long low dam
of sandbags waterproofed with dark blue sheeting
and set a pump to lift leaked waters back
out of the empty to the brimming end.
Mudflats of decomposing sludge appear
below the dam, and notices shout warnings
of Quicksands! Rotting wonderloaf and duckshit.
It's all much shallower than we had thought
even when, last July, opaque green soup
receded from bald banks, and swamp exhaled
such halitosis that we were amazed
that goslings, cygnets, ducklings, could grow up
on algae stew in Piccadilly's barnyard.

   Amphibious men in Council overalls
control machines that scrape the drying mud
out of its concrete bed. It is as though
a woman who has charmed us all our lives
lay in a public operating theatre
to be eviscerated for her health
and ours, so secret workings are exposed
and we discover that our old acquaintance,
who seemed so beautiful, is all prosthetic.
Under her glittering surface, metal pipes
carry the Palace sewage to the Thames.
Her islets are all falsies, and her fountains
that turned green water to white ostrich plumes
were rooted in a fan of metal spouts.
The rocks where pelicans would preen and doze
are borrowed props from some stage grotto scene,
synthetic to the core.

   We think we shall not be deceived again,
but when live water raises its bright mirror
so that the shallow basin fills with trees
grown upside-down, towards a nether sky
where stiff grey fish swim past at a great depth
while growling overhead;

and evening, when it comes, lamplights those fires
that flicker, unextinguished, under water,
with orange flames that make the moon more silver,
then we forget that we were disillusioned
with Lady Lake, the concrete-bottomed beauty.

CHISWICK TIME-PIECE

Full circle and full circle: ticking truths
   add up to one big lie.
   time-circles never meet, but say Goodbye

     quite ruthlessly.

Tame trees mark time, waiting to cross the street
   for more than fifty years.
   They drop their fever-spotted petal tears

     and truthfully

tell us that skipping maidens turn to girls
   with lovers, husbands, prams,
   grey hair in blossomtime, then zimmer-frames.

     Less youthfully

each year, we pace the pavements, and the gardens
   go through their repertoire –
   magnolia and may, wisteria –

     while sapwood hardens.

THE OUTDOOR ROOM

Walls on three sides, with windows into shadow,
shelter my tiny but tree-furnished garden,
and, closing up this alcove, a high fence
dams back the sunrise, keeps a reservoir
of morning dazzle on its eastern side
until it spills and splashes through tree branches
onto the parquet of my brick-paved room.
And to this space, this small suburban space,
the universe comes visiting each day.
And to these days, this summer day, this now,
comes history, coiled in its hiding place;
not even ignorance can keep us safe.

I need not know what lies beyond the fence.
There's nothing of much moment: other gardens,
alleyways, a carpark. Crashing glass
means the well-meaning bottlebank. The traffic,
growling westward, goes to Somerset,
and the embankment to the south of us
supports both District Line and Piccadilly –
now overground and racing to Heathrow.
The river's curve, beyond the Chiswick High Road,
contains this area, shaped like an udder
hung on the old Bath Road. Above its map
grey jets glance down on nowhere of importance.

Thin clouds obscure the aircraft: slow grey fish
drift overhead, changing at night to dragons
with emeralds and rubies in their tails.
The moon is caught and cullissed in the baytree
that struggles with the gale beyond the wall:
it reassembles, free, above the roofridge,
to stare, amazedly, into my garden.
Here we are mortal, everything is mortal
and therefore of great worth. I never know
what treasure may be tossed over the fence:
the moon, a ball, small birds, the raucous jay,
or bruising apples dropped by our own tree.

In early Spring, the quince wears muted scarlet
petals the colour of the silk pyjamas
my father gave my mother in the Thirties,
hoping the ardent colour might warm up
her frightened sexuality. It didn't.
I could unlock my childhood with such keys.
Now polka-dots of appleblossom petals
pattern the mossy ground. If this were all –
this ragged butterfly, that sievelike ceiling –
this outdoor room could be the needle's eye
for all experience to be dragged through.
Its insignificance would be enough.

GENIUS LOCI

The vendor gave no warning, naturally.
We went to view his house, he showed it to us;
he wasn't offering his next-door neighbour.
So when we came with keys to take possession,
Emmeline surprised us.
She leant out from what should have been a roof
and said Don't buy it, don't buy it from him.
We have already bought it we replied.
Then, from the walltop, she poured grievances:
told us that he had tried to steal her garden,
blocked her view with fences, stolen light.
And then she had been firebombed, so she said,
by would-be property developers.
But she stayed on, under her broken roof
and the bay-laurel planted at her birth,
grown up to a green tenement of birds.

One summer day she paid a formal call,
wearing a long white dress, a big straw hat
draped in a chiffon scarf, and cotton gloves.
She sipped a glass of water, and confided:
Before the fire my second husband paid
the rent. I could not pay Electric Bills.
I simply do not know how one makes money.
After the fire she wouldn't move away
but camped among the ruins, sifting ash.
She sorted her charred sketchbooks, covered up,
with plastic sheeting, sculpture by her father
whose workshop it had been. I am, she said,
the Last Indigenous Chiswickian.
It may have been her candles fired the place,
but in those greedy years the site alone,
of her old studio, was worth a bomb.

She comes and goes in Winter, comes to stay
in Summertime; sits under her bay-laurel
teaching her granddaughter to read and count.
She reared four children. Most Important Work,
she said when she called round, and I concurred.
She moved me, but won't speak to me these days
because I said she might have squatters' rights
to fight the machinations of the Council.
She took offence, thinking I meant to mean
the Last Indigenous Chiswickian –
who grew here – was a squatter.
I should have called it 'negative possession'.

One freezing day she climbed the hidden ladder
and leant out from what should have been a roof
to stare reproachfully at my dark windows.
I was no better than the other upstarts
who think they own the Earth.
If she forgives me I would like to tell her
that flickering candle-light and drifting woodsmoke –
meaning she has come home by bicycle
and climbed the carpark fence into her garden,
scorning Chubb locks, security alarms
and all our title deeds – can soothe my sense
of exile from the outgrown place she keeps.

SWIFT SEASON

Scattered cohorts of innocent bees
rummage the frothy meadowsweet plumes,
searching, searching for fugitive treasure,
packing their whiskery thighs with gold.

Rising and falling like fur-bellied crotchets,
they hum the bass that underlines
the shriller-than-treble hooligan choir
of distant screamers overhead

panicking me into consciousness
of Summer's flight, which is swifter than swifts
that circle the sky in excited swarms
of high soprano topnotes, being

international prima donnas
in midsummer's opera. From the wings
I hear the flypast of too many summers
whirring away and vanishing.

Few can be left. The meadowsweet fades
and tarnishes to sober seed, as
fledgeling swifts perfect their flight
on long dark blades, before they leave,

while something within me stands and grieves
for migrant years. I am possessed
by dread of winter and being dead:
timelust, not to be satisfied.

THE SELF PORTRAIT

I thought to draw my living mask,
　　with lines, or light and dark,
so propped a glass up on my desk
　　and made a charcoal mark.

But in the ground below my room –
　　deep in the shadow-well –
a narrow desert longed to bloom
　　and so I left my cell

and softly, down the spiral stair,
　　crept to a bolted door
and, stepping out into the air,
　　proceeded to explore.

Laurels intensified the shade;
　　I pruned and thinned, then found
green ferns, and planted more, I made
　　small areas of ground

by prising up the trodden stones
　　and digging deep; I fed
manure, dried blood and crumbled bones
　　into the barren bed

then sought out flowers to make bright
　　the semidarkness; most
were toxic as the aconite
　　or pallid as a ghost,

but all took root and grew. Pale fire
　　shone in the gloom; bile-green
proliferated; nightshade bore
　　black phials of atropine.

The belladonna that arrests
　　man's heart, grew tall and thrived,
and henbane, on forbidden lists
　　of killers, I reprieved.

When I had climbed the secret stair
and sat again, and drew,
my smiling likeness hinted where
the true self-portrait grew.

INTENSIVE CARE, IN THE CARDIAC UNIT

Like chrysalids that may contain a soul
or may be empty shells, they lie and breathe
on ventilators, so this nursery
may be the mortuary's anteroom
or tortuous passage from the underworld
into the upper air.
Rapt watchers tend half-dead and half-alive
unconscious sleepers who, perhaps, have died
and been preserved in ice a hundred years.
Their hearts are chilled
to check the clock of life, to still
its obstinately flapping frantic fish
to cold passivity, quiescent flesh
which surgeons patch and stitch.
These patients are returning from the dark –
the very bottom of the shadow-well.
Now sense and memory come glimmering back
to surface slowly through a shoal of dreams.
Their hands are white with cold, their faces white,
but graphic glow-worms write above each bed
that hearts beat independently, and breath
oxygenates the blood. All through the night
the body's heat ascends to ninety-eight
point four, or more or less. This is not death.
Eyes open, recognise, refill with black,
preferring to retreat into the dark
and nurse the violated body's hurt:
the sternum sawn, the casket of curved bones
wrenched open, and the busybody hands
invading the locked chest
to heal, not to despoil, and yet
it looks like torture, or blood sacrifice
to buy a span of years, to buy more time.
A living heart is handled at some risk:
across the ward a staring, lifesize doll
is kept alive: but does she know she lives?
Others are luckier, they can clench hands

and curl their toes; their limbs obey
and will transport them back to common day
with death deferred ten years, a hundred moons,
uncounted sunrises away.